Reach
HIGHER

Practice Book

NATIONAL
GEOGRAPHIC
LEARNING

Australia · Brazil · Mexico · Singapore · United Kingdom · United States

National Geographic Learning,
a Cengage Company

Reach Higher Practice Book 1B

Publisher, Content-based English: Erik Gundersen

Associate Director, R&D: Barnaby Pelter

Senior Development Editors:
  Jacqueline Eu
  Ranjini Fonseka
  Kelsey Zhang

Development Editor: Rayne Ngoi

Director of Global Marketing: Ian Martin

Heads of Regional Marketing:
  Charlotte Ellis (Europe, Middle East and Africa)
  Kiel Hamm (Asia)
  Irina Pereyra (Latin America)

Product Marketing Manager: David Spain

Senior Production Controller: Tan Jin Hock

Senior Media Researcher (Covers): Leila Hishmeh

Senior Designer: Lisa Trager

Director, Operations: Jason Seigel

Operations Support:
  Rebecca Barbush
  Drew Robertson
  Caroline Stephenson
  Nicholas Yeaton

Manufacturing Planner: Mary Beth Hennebury

Publishing Consultancy and Composition:
  MPS North America LLC

For permission to use material from this text or product, submit all requests online at **cengage.com/permissions**
Further permissions questions can be emailed to
permissionrequest@cengage.com

ISBN-13: 978-0-357-36657-8

National Geographic Learning
200 Pier Four Blvd
Boston, MA 02210
USA

Locate your local office at **international.cengage.com/region**

Visit National Geographic Learning online at **ELTNGL.com**
Visit our corporate website at **www.cengage.com**

Printed in the United States of America
Print Number: 11   Print Year: 2025

Contents

Unit 5: Creature Features

Unit 6: Up in the Air

Unit 7: Then and Now

Unit 8: Get Out the Map!

Name _____ Date _____

Creature Features

Make a concept map with the answers to the Big Question: How are animals different from one another?

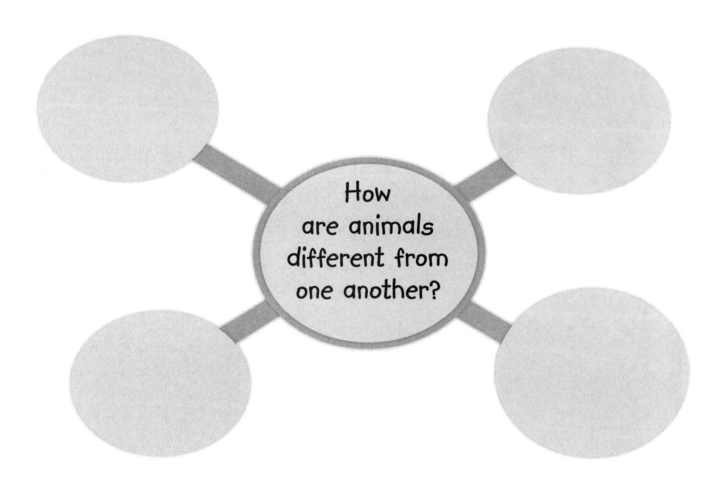

How are animals different from one another?

© Cengage Learning, Inc.

Thinking Map

Compare and Contrast Animals

Choose two animals. Compare and contrast the animals in the Venn diagram.

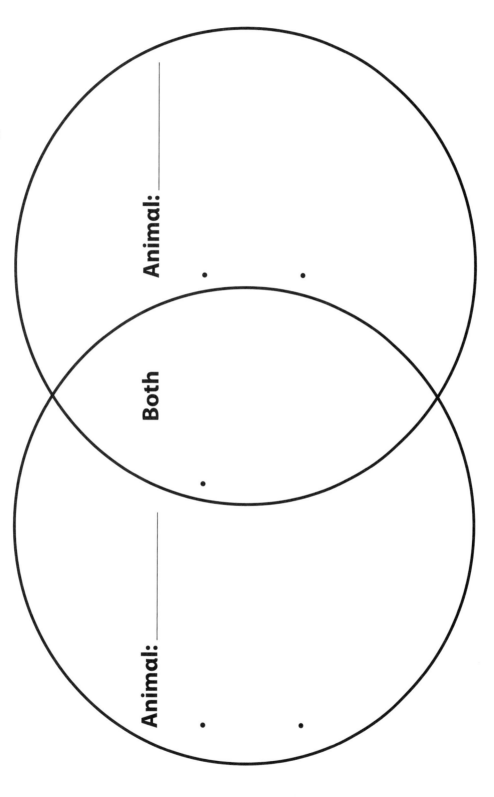

Animal: _____

Both

Animal: _____

Grammar

Name That Part

Grammar Rules Sentences

A sentence has a underlined naming part and a underlined telling part.

Example: *The bear* *swims*.

Circle the naming parts. Underline the telling parts.

1. (The dog) barks.

2. A bird sings.

3. My cat runs.

4. The alligator walks.

5. A rabbit hops.

Choose one of the naming parts above. Add a telling part. Read your sentence to a partner.

"For Pete's Sake"

Listen as your teacher reads. Follow with your finger.

1

Pete was green. He wanted to be pink like everyone else. The others told him he just wasn't ripe yet.

2

Pete had four feet and no feathers. Everyone else had two feet and feathers. Nothing could make Pete feel happy.

3

Then some strangers arrived. They looked like Pete. He felt very happy.

4

Pete told the others he was different. He was the same, too. They told him that he always had been.

Grammar

Can You See It?

Grammar Rules Sentence Capitalization

1. Sentences begin with a **capital letter**.
2. Sentences end with an **end mark**.

Example: *The alligator swims.*

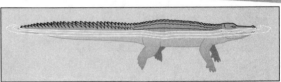

Read the group of words. Write each group as a sentence.
Use a capital letter and a period.

1. i see an alligator

I see an alligator.

2. it has scales

_____

- -

_____

3. it hides in tall grass

_____

- -

_____

Read one of the sentences. Ask a partner to point to the capital letter and the end mark.

Vocabulary Bingo

Play Bingo using the Key Words from this unit.

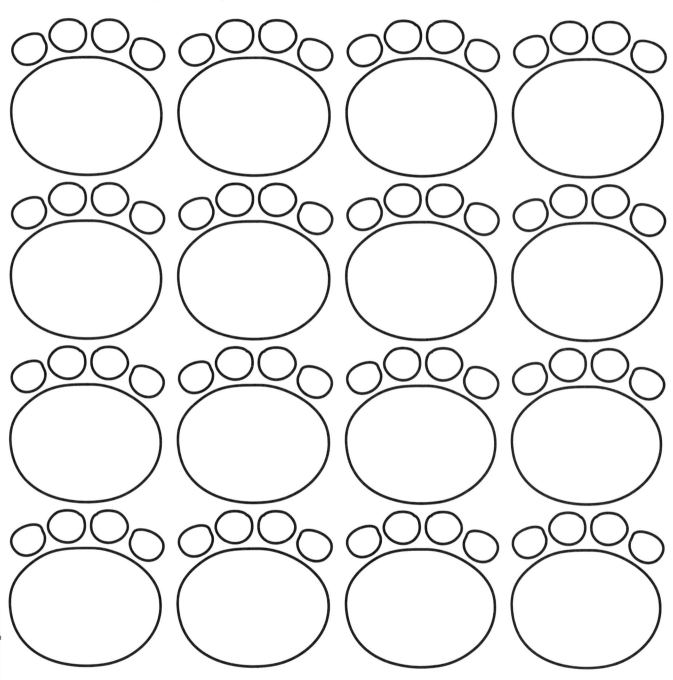

Reread and Retell

"For Pete's Sake"

Compare Pete and Pete's friends.

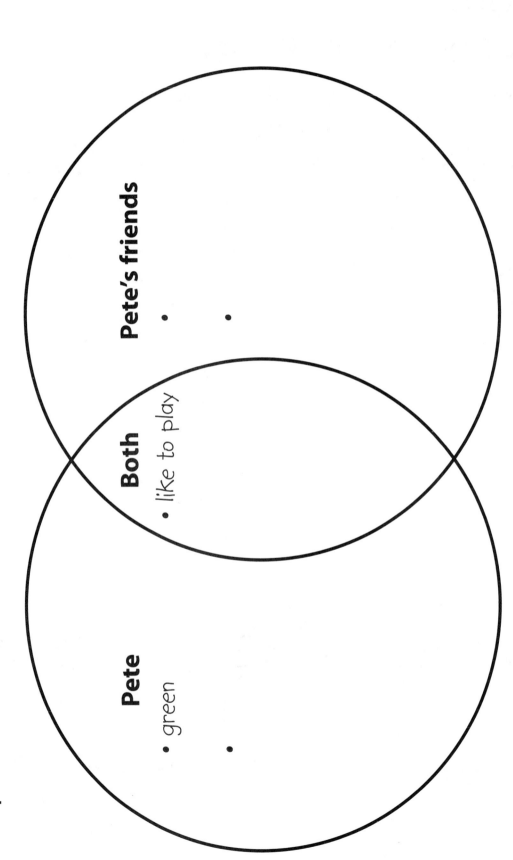

Pete's friends
- •
- •

Both
- like to play

Pete
- green
- •

Take turns with a partner. Use your Venn diagram to tell about Pete and Pete's friends.

Long *u* spelled *u_e, ue*

cube   fuel

Read each word. Circle the word that goes with each picture.

1. cute cut	**2.** rest rescue
3. statue state	**4.** met mute
5. us mule	**6.** argue artist

Work with a partner. Take turns reading and answering the question.

What can you use to rescue a cute puppy?

Name _____ Date _____

"For Pete's Sake"

Use this passage to practice reading with proper expression.

"Stop!" said the others, laughing. 5

"You're getting our feathers wet." 10

Uh-oh. Pete didn't have any feathers. 16

From "For Pete's Sake," page 20

Compare Genres

Compare an animal fantasy and a science article.

Animal fantasy	Science article
no labels	has labels

Tell a partner how an animal fantasy and a science article are different.

Grammar

Build a Sentence Game

Grammar Rules Complete Sentences

A complete sentence has a <u>naming part</u> and a <u>telling part</u>.

- Start a sentence with a **capital letter**.
- End a sentence with an **end mark**.

Example: **A** *tiger has paws.*

1. Toss a marker onto one of the sentence parts below.

2. Put it together with another sentence part to make a complete sentence.

3. Write the complete sentence on a separate piece of paper.

4. Say the sentence to a partner.

the monkey			the elephant
has a tail			the giraffe
can run			has fur
can climb			the tiger
the snake			has a mouth

Thinking Map

Categorize Movements

Add animals and their movements to the category chart.

Animals	Movement
fish turtles	swim
	fly
	run

Grammar

Cat Naps

Grammar Rules Simple Subject

1. The naming part of a sentence is called the **subject** of the sentence.
2. The **subject** tells who or what the sentence is about.

Example: **The bird** hops. **It** sings a song.

Circle the naming part in each sentence.

1. The cat naps.

2. It rests.

3. The puppy plays.

4. Kit wakes up.

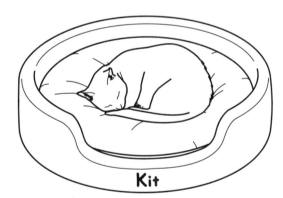

Kit

5. They run and jump.

 **Choose a sentence above. Change the naming part. Say the new sentence to a partner.**

Name _____   Date _____

"Slither, Slide, Hop, and Run"

Listen as your teacher reads. Follow with your finger.

1

Birds fly through the air with wings. Snakes slither from side to side on the ground.

2

Horses run. They move their legs forward and backward. Kangaroos hop. They use their back feet. Snails slide slowly on the ground.

3

Dolphins swim. They move their tails up and down. Dogs dig. They move dirt with their paws. Raccoons climb. They move their feet up and down.

Match Sentence Parts

Grammar Rules Simple Predicate

1. The telling part of a sentence is called the **predicate** of the sentence.

2. The **predicate** can tell what the subject does.

Example: *The kitten* **sits**.

1. Read the sentence parts below. Match a naming part with a telling part to make a sentence.

2. Write the sentence on a separate piece of paper. Circle the telling part.

The cat	The puppy
can run.	The monkey
jumps.	can swim.
is happy.	She
digs.	A dog

Read one of your sentences to a partner. Say the telling part.

Vocabulary

Rivet

Play a game by filling in the letters of each word.

1. For each word, write the first letter given by your teacher.

2. Listen to a sentence and guess the missing word.

3. Fill in the other letters of the word.

1. ___ ___ ___ ___

2. ___ ___ ___

3. ___ ___ ___ ___ ___ ___ ___ ___

4. ___ ___ ___ ___

5. ___ ___ ___

6. ___ ___ ___ ___ ___

7. ___ ___ ___ ___ ___ ___

8. ___ ___ ___ ___ ___ ___

9. ___ ___ ___ ___ ___

10. ___ ___ ___ ___ ___ ___

11. ___ ___ ___ ___ ___ ___ ___ ___

Name _____   Date _____

"Slither, Slide, Hop, and Run"

Categorize the animals and their movements in "Slither, Slide, Hop, and Run."

Animals	Movement
birds bats	fly
horses	

▬▬▬ **Work with a partner. Use your category chart to summarize the information in the reading selection.**

Phonics Practice

Sounds and Spellings: *ge, gi, dge*

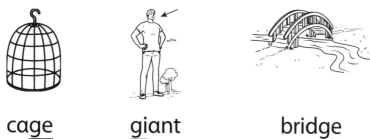

cage   giant   bridge

Read each word. Circle the word that goes with each picture.

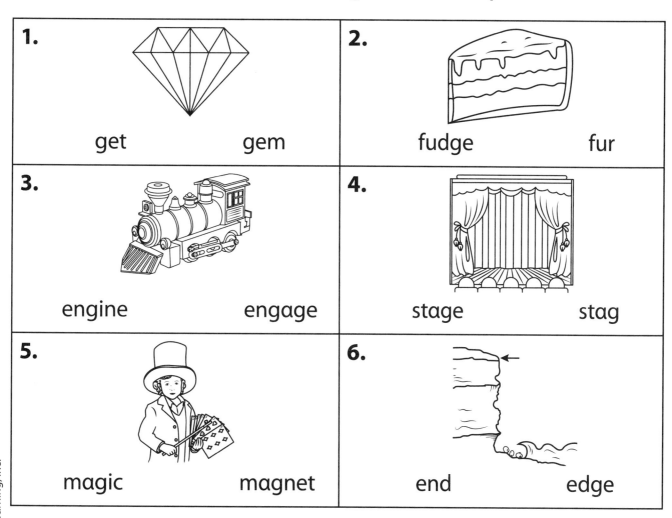

1.	2.
get gem	fudge fur
3.	**4.**
engine engage	stage stag
5.	**6.**
magic magnet	end edge

Work with a partner. Take turns reading the sentence and pointing to the objects.

Find an engine, a gem, and fudge.

Fluency

"Slither, Slide, Hop, and Run"

Use this passage to practice reading with the proper intonation.

A kangaroo can hop! It makes short   7

leaps into the air. It uses its back feet   16

to hop.   18

A horse can run! Its legs move forward   26

and backward very quickly.   30

From "Slither, Slide, Hop, and Run," pages 52–53

Intonation

B ☐ Does not change pitch.   A ☐ Changes pitch to match some of the content.

I ☐ Changes pitch, but does not match content.   AH ☐ Changes pitch to match all of the content.

Accuracy and Rate Formula

Use the formula to measure a reader's accuracy and rate while reading aloud.

_____ − _____ = _____
words attempted   number of errors   words correct per
in one minute   minute (wcpm)

Compare Genres

Use a Venn diagram to compare a fact book and a photo journal.

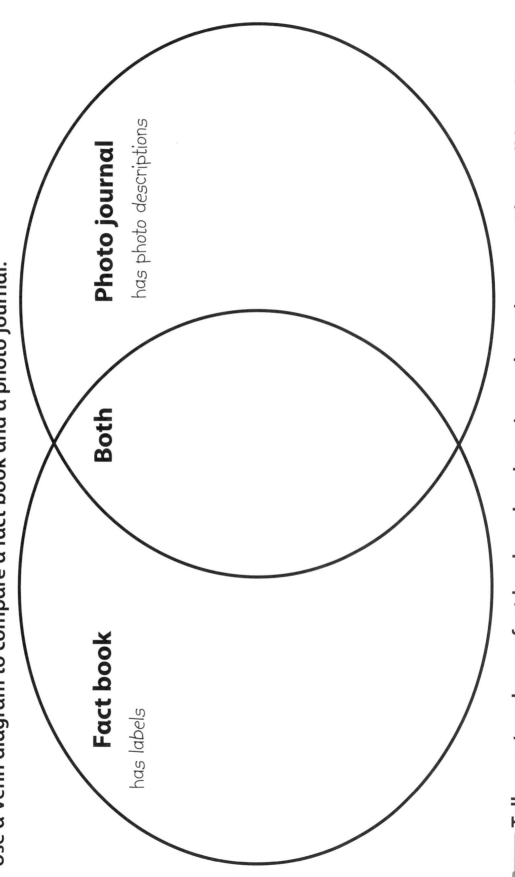

Fact book

has labels

Both

Photo journal

has photo descriptions

Tell a partner how a fact book and a photo journal are the same. Then tell how they are different.

Name _____ Date _____

Let's Swim

Grammar Rules Subject-Verb Agreement

1. If the subject names one, use **s** at the end of the verb.
2. If the subject names more than one, do not use **s** at the end of the verb.

Choose the verb that goes with the subject. Write the sentence.

1. One fish (swim/swims).

One fish swims.

2. Two fish (swim/swims).

_____

_____

3. A fish (come/comes) here.

_____

_____

4. Many fish (come/comes) here.

_____

_____

Pick a verb from above. Write a new sentence. Read it to a partner.

Writing Project

Voice

Every writer has a special way of saying things, or a voice. The voice should sound genuine, or real, and be unique to that writer.

	Does the tone, formal or informal, fit the purpose and audience?	Does the writing sound genuine to the writer?
4 Wow!	❑ The writer's tone fits the purpose and audience.	❑ The writing is genuine. It shows who the writer is.
3 Ahh.	❑ The writer's tone mostly fits the purpose and audience.	❑ Most of the writing sounds genuine.
2 Hmm.	❑ Some of the writing fits the purpose and audience. Some does not.	❑ Some of the writing sounds genuine.
1 Huh?	❑ The writer's tone does not fit the purpose and audience.	❑ The writing does not sound genuine.

Writing Project

Main Idea and Details Chart

Complete the chart for your article.

The main idea:

Supporting detail:

Supporting detail:

Supporting detail:

Revise

Use revision marks to make changes to this paragraph. Look for:

- a main idea
- details that tell more about the main idea
- complete sentences

Revision Marks	
∧	Add
℘	Take out
⌒⌐	Move to here

A lion is the loudest cat ever. Its roar is heard mostly at night.

My favorite cat is the cheetah. A lion's roar can be heard from miles

away. Loud cat Dogs are loud, too.

Writing Project

Edit and Proofread

Use revision marks to edit and
proofread this paragraph. Look for:

- complete sentences
- subject-verb agreement
- capitalization and end punctuation
- correct spelling of long vowel words
  with silent *e*

Revision Marks	
∧	Add
ℛ	Take out
⬯⤹	Move to here
⬯ *SP*	Check spelling
≡	Capitalize
⊙	Add a period

grizzly bears sleeps all winter. First, they dig a den Then they

crawl in and go to slep. Like to sleep!

Up in the Air

Make a concept map with the answers to the Big Question:
What's wild about weather?

What's wild about weather?

Find Cause and Effect

Explain what happens when it rains all day. Write the effects in the cause-and-effect chart.

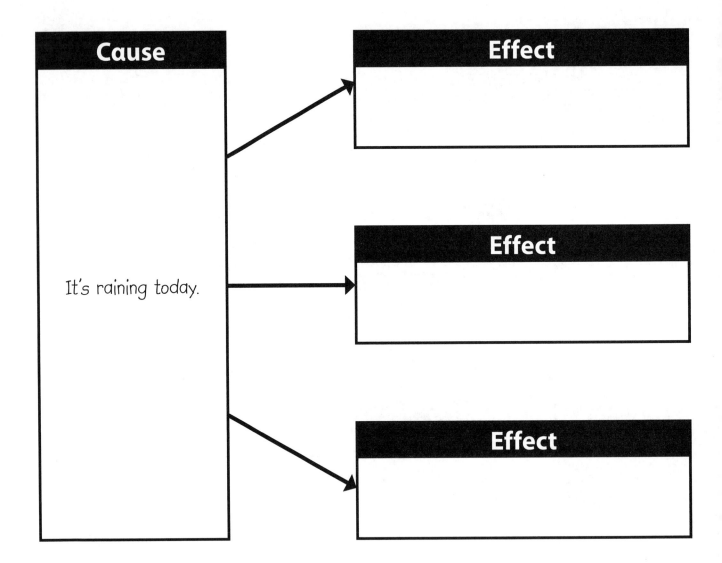

Cause

It's raining today.

Effect

Effect

Effect

Grammar

Weather Report

Grammar Rules Statements, Exclamations, and Commands

Sentence Type	What It Does	How It Ends
statement	tells something	.
exclamation	tells something with strong feeling	!
command	tells someone to do something	. or !

1. With a partner, read the sentences.
2. Write *statement, exclamation,* or *command* next to each sentence.
3. The first pair to complete the activity correctly wins.

1. It is stormy.

statement

2. Bring your umbrella.

3. It is very wet!

4. It is windy.

 Take turns with a partner. Say the sentences.

© Cengage Learning, Inc.

Name _____   Date _____

"I Face the Wind"

Listen as your teacher reads. Follow with your finger.

1

The wind is very strong. You can't see it but you can feel it. You can see what it does to flags, trees, and other things.

2

You can catch the air. You can make your own wind, too.

3

The wind is made of air. The fastest winds are called tornadoes. One of the softest winds is your breath. Face the wind. Feel it push you.

Grammar

No, He Is Not

Grammar Rules Negative Sentences/Questions

Some **questions** can be answered with **Yes** or **No**.

- Start these questions with **Do**, **Does**, **Is**, **Are**, or **Can**.
- Use **no** and **not** for a negative answer.

Example: ***Are*** *you ten years old?*

   No, *I am* ***not*** *ten years old.*

Read the question. Look at the pictures. Then answer the question.

1. Is he wearing a hat?

No, he is not wearing a hat.

2. Does he have a coat?

_____

- - - - - - - - - - - - - - - - - -

_____

3. Is she wearing a sweater?

_____

- - - - - - - - - - - - - - - - - -

_____

4. Can she see snow?

_____

- - - - - - - - - - - - - - - - - -

_____

Ask a partner a question about one of the pictures. Have your partner give a negative answer.

Vocabulary

Picture It

1. Form pairs. Choose a pair to be the artists and a pair to be the guessers.

2. The artists secretly select a Key Word.

3. The artists draw a picture to show the word's meaning.

4. The guessers have to guess which Key Word the picture shows.

5. Switch roles.

KEY WORDS

weather	storm	blow	feel	soft
wind	fast	strong	outside	power

1.	2.
3.	**4.**

Keeping Score
If the guessers answer correctly, they get one point.
The first pair to get three points wins!

Reread and Retell

"I Face the Wind"

Use the cause-and-effect chart to explain the effects
of the wind in the story.

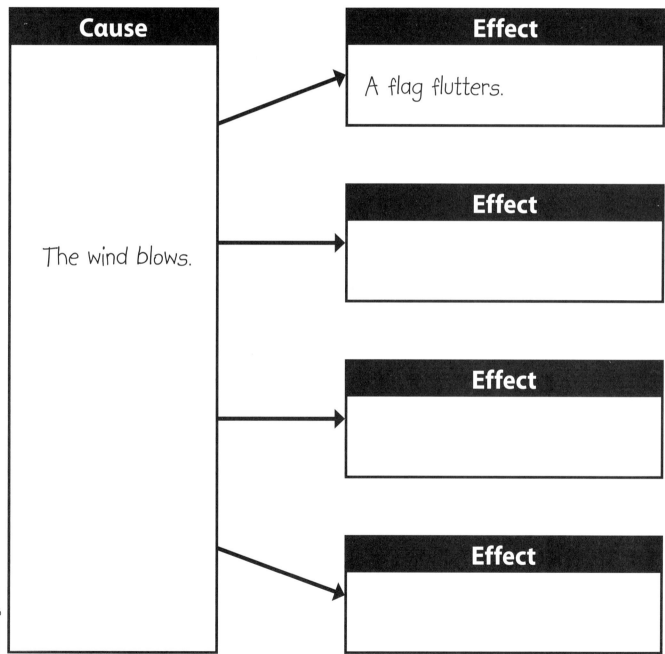

Cause
The wind blows.

Effect

A flag flutters.

Effect

Effect

Effect

Use your cause-and-effect chart to tell a partner facts you
learned about the wind in "I Face the Wind."

Phonics Practice

Sounds and Spellings: *ce, ci*

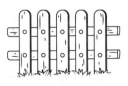
fen__ce__

__ci__rcus

Read each word. Circle the word that goes with each picture.

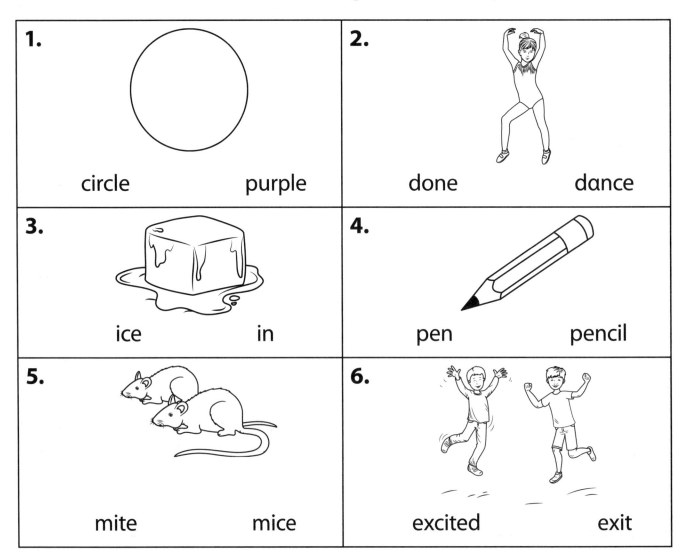

1. circle purple	**2.** done dance
3. ice in	**4.** pen pencil
5. mite mice	**6.** excited exit

Work with a partner. Take turns reading and answering the question.

Are you excited to see mice dance?

_____

Fluency

"I Face the Wind"

Use this passage to practice reading with proper expression.

1 Open a large plastic bag.   6

Make sure there are no holes in it.   14

2 Pull the bag through the air so it puffs up.   25

3 Twist it closed to trap the air you caught.   35

4 Squeeze the bag to feel the air.   43

From "I Face The Wind," pages 92–93

Expression

| B | ☐ Does not read with feeling. | A | ☐ Reads with appropriate feeling for most content. |
| I | ☐ Reads with some feeling, but does not match content. | AH | ☐ Reads with appropriate feeling for all content. |

Accuracy and Rate Formula

Use the formula to measure a reader's accuracy and rate while reading aloud.

$$\underline{\hspace{3cm}} - \underline{\hspace{3cm}} = \underline{\hspace{3cm}}$$

| words attempted in one minute | number of errors | words correct per minute (wcpm) |

Respond and Extend

Character's Actions

Use a two-column chart to read Gluscabi's actions. Write the reason for his actions in the chart.

Gluscabi's actions	Reasons
Gluscabi went to see Wind Eagle.	There was too much wind. Gluscabi couldn't fish.
Gluscabi put Wind Eagle in a hole.	
Gluscabi went to see Wind Eagle again.	
Gluscabi took Wind Eagle out of the hole.	

Choose one of Gluscabi's actions. With a partner, share Gluscabi's reason.

Outside

Grammar Rules Sentence Types

1. A **statement** tells something.
2. A **question** asks something.
3. An **exclamation** shows strong feeling.
4. A **command** tells someone to do something.

You can play outside in the park today. Work with a partner to write about it.

1. Write a statement that tells what you can do in the park.

I can ride my bike.

2. Write a question about the park.

3. Tell your friend to bring something to the park.

4. Write to show how you feel about playing in the park.

Classify Details

Use a classification chart to classify activities people do in different kinds of weather.

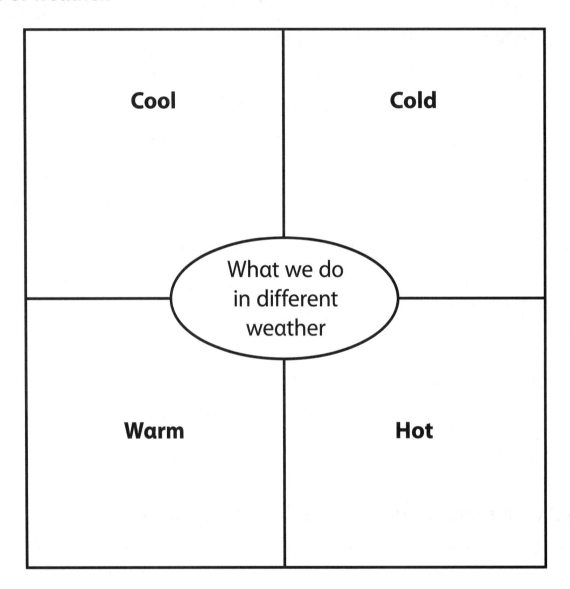

Cool

Cold

What we do in different weather

Warm

Hot

Grammar

Make a Match

Grammar Rules Yes/No Questions

Yes/No questions begin with a verb.

- Answer with **Yes** or **No**.
- Use the same verb in the answer.

Example: **Is** it cloudy?

 Yes, it **is** cloudy.

1. Partner 1 points to a Question Card.

2. Partner 2 points to an Answer Card.

3. If the question and the answer match, cross out both cards.

4. Play until all the cards are crossed out.

Question Cards	
Is it snowing?	Is it windy?
Is it sunny?	Is it raining?

Answer Cards	
No, it is not windy.	Yes, it is raining.
Yes, it is sunny.	No, it is not snowing.

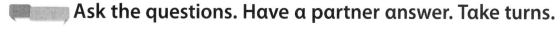 Ask the questions. Have a partner answer. Take turns.

Key Points Reading

"A Year for Kiko"

Listen as your teacher reads. Follow with your finger.

1

January	**February**	**March**
Snow is falling on Kiko.	Kiko's window is cold and white.	Wind blows Kiko's hair.

2

April	**May**	**June**
Rain falls on the earth.	Kiko plants a seed.	Kiko picks strawberries.

3

July	**August**	**September**
Kiko chases fireflies.	It is hot. Kiko swims to get cool.	Crickets sing.

4

October	**November**	**December**
Red and gold leaves are falling.	Kiko looks for the moon.	Kiko wears her coat, mittens, and hat.

Who? What? Where?

Grammar Rules Question Words

Start a question with a **question word**.

Examples: *who, what, where, when, why, how*

Use *who, when, where, why,* or *how* to complete the questions.

1. __Who__ has an umbrella?

2. _____ can we build a snowman?

3. _____ is my hat?

4. _____ cold is it outside?

5. _____ is it so hot?

Write a new question using one of the question words. Ask a partner your question.

Vocabulary

Rivet

Play a game by filling in the letters of each word.

1. For each word, write the first letter given by your teacher.
2. Listen to a sentence and guess the missing word.
3. Fill in the other letters of the word.

1. __ __ __ __ __

2. __ __ __ __ __

3. __ __ __ __

4. __ __ __ __ __ __ __ __ __ __

5. __ __ __ __ __ __

6. __ __ __ __ __ __ __

7. __ __ __ __ __ __ __ __

8. __ __ __ __ __

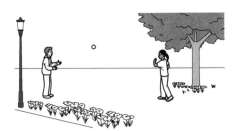

9. __ __ __ __ __ __

10. __ __ __ __ __ __

11. __ __ __ __ __

12. __ __ __ __ __

⬛⬛⬛ **Take turns with a partner. Choose a word. Say it in a sentence.**

Name _____ Date _____

"A Year for Kiko"

Add details to the classification chart about things Kiko does in different weather.

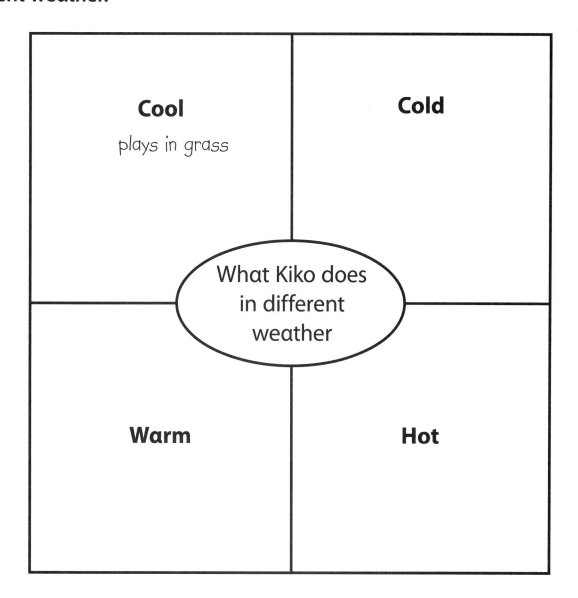

Cool

plays in grass

Cold

What Kiko does in different weather

Warm

Hot

Retell "A Year for Kiko" to a partner. Use your chart and illustrations in the story.

Sounds and Spellings: *ch, tch, wh*

c<u>h</u>air

wa<u>tch</u>

<u>wh</u>eel

Read each word. Circle the word that goes with each picture.

1.	child called wild	**2.**	hip ship whip
3.	hat hatch has	**4.**	wheat heat seat
5.	hair chin chain	**6.**	crust itch crush

Work with a partner. Take turns reading the sentence and pointing to the objects.

Point to a child, a whip, and a chair.

Name _____   Date _____

Fluency

"A Year for Kiko"

Use this passage to practice reading with proper expression.

In December Kiko breathes out clouds.   6

She puts on her winter coat.   12

She wears her mittens and hat.   18

Kiko is ready for snow.   23

From "A Year for Kiko," page 132

Expression

B ☐ Does not read with feeling.

A ☐ Reads with appropriate feeling for most content.

I ☐ Reads with some feeling, but does not match content.

AH ☐ Reads with appropriate feeling for all content.

Accuracy and Rate Formula

Use the formula to measure a reader's accuracy and rate while reading aloud.

_____ − _____ = _____
words attempted   number of errors   words correct per
in one minute   minute (wcpm)

Respond and Extend

Compare Genres

Use a T chart to compare a story and an interview.

Realistic fiction	Interview
has characters	has real people

 Use your T chart to talk about which kind of text you like best. Give reasons.

Grammar

Who? What? Where?

Grammar Rules Ask Questions

Question Words	Information
Who	person
Where	place
What	thing or action
Why	reason
When	time
How	way something is done

Circle the question word. Then write the type of information it gives. Choose from *person, place, thing, reason, time,* or *way something is done.*

1. (When) are we going ice skating?  time

2. Where is the park? - - - - - - - - - - - -

3. What should I bring? - - - - - - - - - -

4. Who is going? - - - - - - - - - - - - -

 Write a new question about the park. Use a question word. Have a partner say the type of information it gives.

Name _____ Date _____

Ideas

Writing is well-developed when the message is clear and interesting to the reader. It is supported by details that show the writer knows the topic well.

	Is the message clear and focused?	Do the details show the writer knows the topic?
4 Wow!	❏ All of the writing is clear and focused.	❏ All the details tell about the topic. The writer knows the topic well.
3 Ahh.	❏ Most of the writing is clear and focused.	❏ Most of the details are about the topic. The writer knows the topic fairly well.
2 Hmm.	❏ Some of the writing is not clear. The writing lacks some focus.	❏ Some details are about the topic. The writer doesn't know the topic well.
1 Huh?	❏ The writing is not clear or focused.	❏ Many details are not about the topic. The writer does not know the topic.

Weather Cause-and-Effects Chart

Write one kind of weather in the left box under **Cause**. Write four things that can happen during that type of weather in the right box under **Effects**.

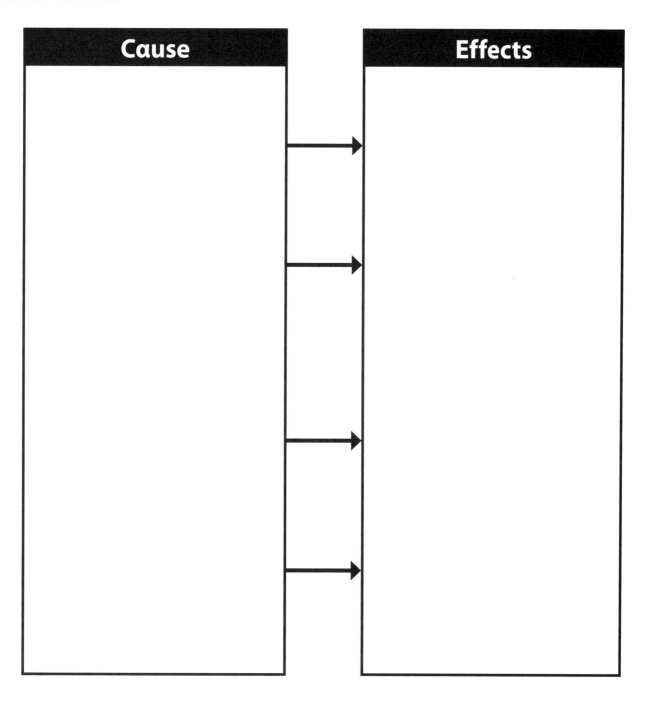

Writing Project

Revise

Use revision marks to make changes to this paragraph. Look for:

- examples to explain the idea windy weather
- vivid or interesting words

Revision Marks	
^	Add
ϑ	Take out
⟋	Move to here

Kites are in the air. Trees bend. These things all happen because

the weather is windy. Leaves fall. The wind goes over the hills.

Edit and Proofread

Use revision marks to edit and proofread this paragraph. Look for:

- **correct spelling of vowel digraphs**
- **missing letters**
- **correct end marks**

Revision Marks	
^	Add
ℱ	Take out
⌒↷	Move to here
◯SP	Check spelling
≡	Capitalize
⊙	Add a period
?	Add a question mark
!	Add an exclamation point

kites dance in the air. Trees bend and sway? Do you hear the

leaves. Whoosh This all happens because the weather is winddy.

The wind blos over the hills.

Name _____   Date _____

Then and Now

Make a concept map with the answers to the Big Question:
What's the difference between then and now?

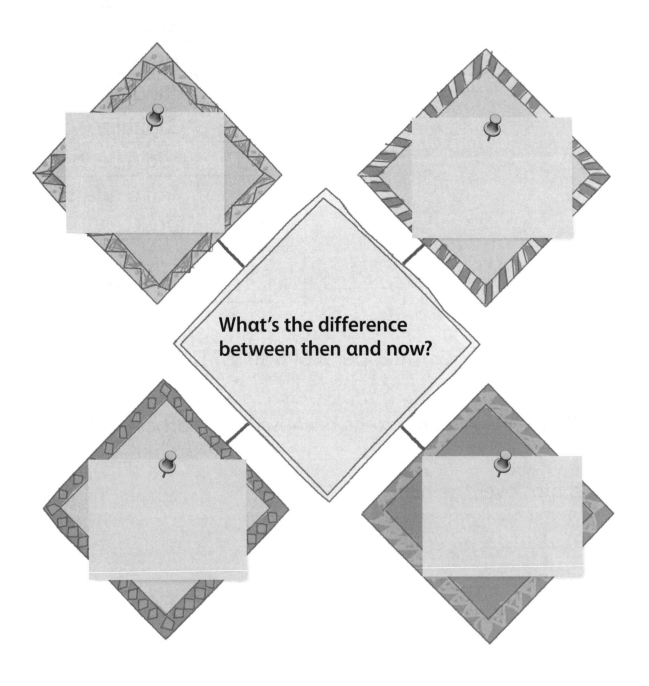

What's the difference
between then and now?

Thinking Map

Identify Main Idea and Details

Complete the diagram. Write different ways people communicate.

People communicate in different ways.

Grammar

What Happened Yesterday?

Grammar Rules Regular Past Tense

Add **-ed** to many action verbs to show that action happened in the past.

Examples: *We **waited** in the rain for an hour.*
*Yesterday I **called** my aunt.*

Read each sentence. Add -ed to each bolded word. Write the new word.

1. I _____mailed_____ a letter. **mail**

2. You _____ me on your cell phone. **call**

3. She _____ the news on TV. **watch**

4. We _____ a game on the computer. **play**

5. They _____ to the radio. **listen**

▬▬▬ Tell a partner about one thing you did yesterday.

7.3 Unit 7 | Then and Now

Name _____ Date _____

"Communication Then and Now"

Listen as your teacher reads. Follow with your finger.

1

Communication is sharing news and ideas. Talking, writing, and body language are all ways to communicate. Communication is now better and faster than in the past.

2

In the past, people copied each book by hand. Now, machines make printed books or e-books. You can read books on computers, too.

3

A long time ago, people sent messages with telegraph machines. Now people call each other on telephones. People also wrote letters in the past. Now people send e-mail messages on computers.

4

People used to get their news by reading newspapers. Many people still have newspapers delivered to their home. But they also read the news online. Communication will continue to change. What will happen next?

Grammar

That Was Then

Grammar Rules Irregular Past Tense Verbs

Some verbs change a lot to tell about the past.

Present	Past
am, is	was
are	were
do	did
go	went

Read each sentence. Circle the correct form of the verb in ( ).

1. My aunt (do, (did)) her homework on paper.

2. Today I (do, did) my homework on the computer.

3. Long ago, people (go, went) by horse.

4. Now, people (go, went) by car.

5. Then, the news (is, was) on the radio.

6. Today, the news (is, was) on the Internet.

Say a sentence using was, were, did, or went to a partner.

Vocabulary

Around the World

Play a game using Key Words.

1. The traveler stands behind a challenger.

2. The challenger listens to the traveler's clue and names the Key Word.

3. The traveler moves behind the next student on the right if the challenger answers correctly. The first traveler to go all around the circle wins.

KEY WORDS

news	computer	message	past	future

CLUES

1. We can send a _____ with e-mail.

2. I have some _____ to share with you about our school.

3. In the _____, I will be an adult.

4. My mom reads e-books on her _____.

5. In the _____, I was a baby.

Reread and Retell

"Communication Then and Now"

Complete the diagram below. Write about how communication has changed.

Communication has changed.

Stories	
Then	**Now**
pictures	words

Messages	
Then	**Now**

News	
Then	**Now**

Use your diagram to retell the article to a partner.

© Cengage Learning, Inc.

Phonics Practice

Digraphs: *sh, th*

shell

feather

Read each word. Circle the word that goes with each picture.

1.		he she the
2.		that hat hit
3.		mother sister brother
4.		shop stop sip
5.		dull dust dish
6.		weather water waiter

Work with a partner. Take turns reading and answering the question.

Can she buy a dish at a shop with her mother and brother?

Fluency

"Communication Then and Now"

Use the passage to practice reading with proper intonation.

Long ago, people copied each book.   6

If they wanted 10 copies of a book, they had   16

to write out each copy one at a time.   25

Now, machines make printed books   30

or e-books. Printed books   34

are made with printing presses.   39

People read e-books on computers.   44

From "Communication Then and Now," pages 160–161

Intonation

B ☐ Does not change pitch.	A ☐ Changes pitch to match some of the content.
I ☐ Changes pitch, but does not match content.	AH ☐ Changes pitch to match all content.

Accuracy and Rate Formula

Use the formula to measure a reader's accuracy and rate while reading aloud.

_____ − _____ = _____
words attempted   number of errors   words correct per
in one minute   minute (wcpm)

Respond and Extend

Compare Genres

Use a Venn diagram to compare a history article and a blog entry.

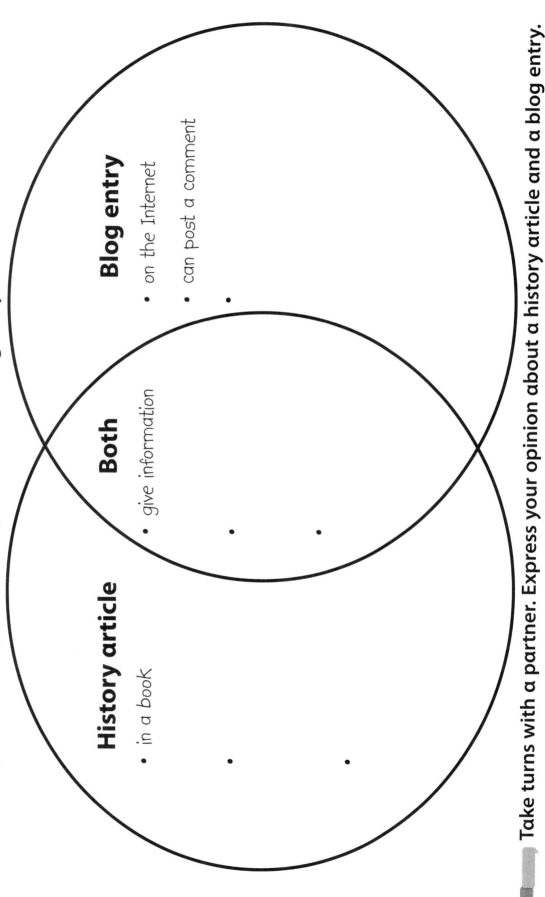

History article
- in a book
- •
- •

Both
- give information
- •
- •

Blog entry
- on the Internet
- can post a comment
- •

Take turns with a partner. Express your opinion about a history article and a blog entry.

Name _____   Date _____

Make It Past Tense

Grammar Rules Past Tense Verbs

To make a **verb** about the **past**:

• Add **-ed** to the end of a regular verb, like *watch*.

• Use the special form of an irregular verb, like *fly*.

1. **Play with a partner.**

2. **Spin the spinner.**

3. **Change the verb to the past tense.**

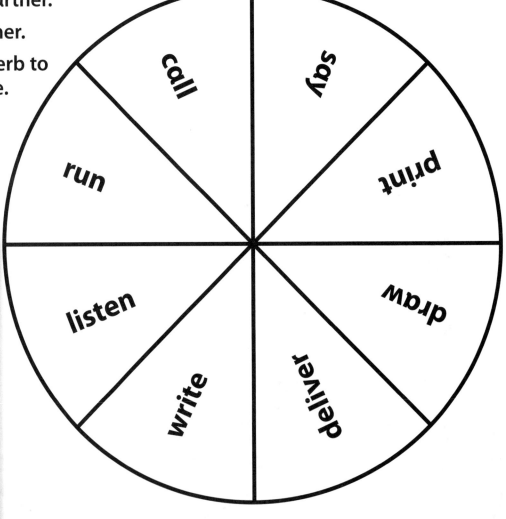

Make a Spinner

1. Place one loop of a paper clip over the center of the circle.

2. Push a sharp pencil through the loop and the paper.

3. Spin the paper clip around the pencil.

Thinking Map

Describe Characters' Feelings

Use a character description chart to list what Marta says or does.
Then describe what this shows about how she feels.

Character	What the character says	What this shows about how the character feels
Marta		

Name _____   Date _____

When?

Grammar Rules Future Tense with *will*

Add **will** in front of a verb to make it **future tense**.

Example: *I **will** call my friend on the phone.*

Read each sentence. Use the correct tense of the bold word to complete the sentence.

1. We _____ will visit _____ our family next week. **visit**

2. They _____ us at the airport yesterday. **meet**

3. We _____ at their house tomorrow. **stay**

4. We _____ to the zoo soon. **go**

5. Last night we _____ a movie. **watch**

6. We _____ ice cream after dinner. **eat**

 Tell a partner what you will do after school today.

"A New Old Tune"

Listen as your teacher reads. Follow with your finger.

1

Max helps **Aunt Nell** get ready for a yard sale. He finds a large disk. Aunt Nell explains that it is a record. She shows him how it plays on a record player.

2

Aunt Nell says **that** things change. She had a black and white TV. She had a phone with a cord.

3

Aunt Nell says that some new things are easier to use. But some things stay the same. People still like to talk on the phone. They like to watch TV, listen to music, and dance.

Grammar

Let's Go!

Grammar Rules Future Tense with *am/is/are going to*	
To make **verbs** about the **future**, add these words before the verb:	

Future	Example
am going to	I *am going to* build a house.
is going to	He *is going to* make a cake.
are going to	You *are going to* invent a machine.

Complete the sentences. Write *am going to*, *is going to*, or *are going to*.

1. Tim  is going to play soccer.

2. Aunt Lin and Mom _____ take a walk.

3. I _____ jump rope.

4. He _____ run a race.

5. You _____ skate.

⬛ With a partner, write sentences about recess. Use *am going to, is going to,* and *are going to.*

Vocabulary

Picture It

1. Form pairs. Choose a pair to be the artists and a pair to be the guessers.

2. The artists secretly select a Key Word.

3. The artists draw a picture to show the word's meaning.

4. The guessers guess which Key Word the picture shows.

5. Switch roles.

KEY WORDS

record	music	better	tool	easier	new
old	invent	machine	build	modern	feel

1.	2.
3.	4.

Keeping Score

If the guessers answer correctly, they get one point.
The first pair to get three points wins!

Name _____   Date _____

"A New Old Tune"

Use a character description chart to list the things Max and Nell say or do. Then describe what this shows about how the character feels.

Character	What the character says or does	What this shows about how the character feels
Max	• Wow •	• He feels surprised. •
Nell	• •	• •

▶ **Use your chart to retell the story to a partner.**

Vowel Sounds and Spellings: *er, ir, ur*

f<u>er</u>n   g<u>ir</u>l   n<u>ur</u>se

Read each word. Circle the word that goes with each picture.

1.	ski slip skirt	**2.**	her him hut
3.	court curl cut	**4.**	tie higher tiger
5.	burst bus dirt	**6.**	first fast fun

Work with a partner. Take turns reading and answering the question.

Does her tiger have a skirt?

Name _____ Date _____

"A New Old Tune"

Use the passage to practice reading with proper expression.

"Has anything stayed the same?" 5

asked Max. 7

"Yes," said Aunt Nell. "People still 13

love to talk on the telephone. And watch 21

television. And listen to music." 26

"And dance!" added Max. 30

From "A New Old Tune," page 199

Expression

B	☐ Does not read with feeling.	A	☐ Reads with appropriate feeling for most content.
I	☐ Reads with some feeling, but does not match content.	AH	☐ Reads with appropriate feeling for all content.

Accuracy and Rate Formula

Use the formula to measure a reader's accuracy and rate while reading aloud.

$$\underline{\hspace{3cm}} - \underline{\hspace{3cm}} = \underline{\hspace{3cm}}$$

words attempted   number of errors   words correct per
in one minute   minute (wcpm)

Respond and Extend

Compare Genres

Use a Venn diagram to compare realistic fiction and poetry.

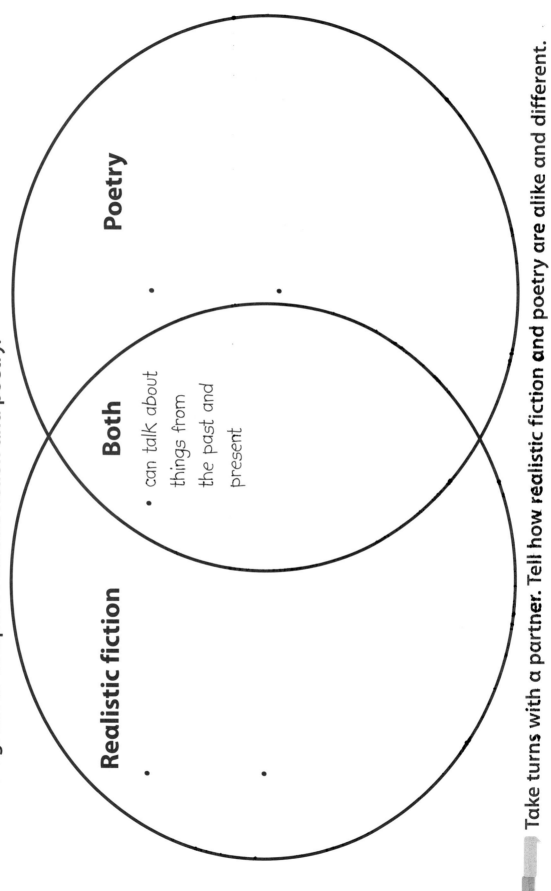

Poetry

Both
- can talk about things from the past and present

Realistic fiction

Take turns with a partner. Tell how realistic fiction and poetry are alike and different.

7.20

Grammar

Make It Happen

Grammar Rules Future Tense Verbs

To make **verbs** about the **future**, add **will, am going to, is going to**, or **are going to** before the verb.

Examples:

*You **will** listen to music.*

*He **is going to** read a book.*

1. Play with a partner.

2. Choose one word from the Future and Verb columns below. Create as many sentences as you can.

3. Cross out the words you choose.

4. Your partner takes a turn.

5. The player who writes the most complete sentences wins.

Future	Verb
will	build
am going to	invent
is going to	make
are going to	write
will	draw

© Cengage Learning, Inc.

Writing Project

Organization

Writing is organized when it is easy to follow. All the ideas make sense together and flow from one idea to the next in an order that fits the writer's audience and purpose.

	Is the writing well-organized? Does it fit the writer's purpose?	Does the writing flow?
4 Wow!	❑ The writing is very well-organized. ❑ It clearly fits the writer's purpose.	❑ The writing is smooth and logical. Each sentence flows into the next one.
3 Ahh.	❑ Most of the writing is organized. ❑ It mostly fits the writer's purpose.	❑ Most of the writing is smooth. There are only a few sentences that do not flow logically.
2 Hmm.	❑ The writing is not well-organized. ❑ It fits the writer's purpose somewhat.	❑ Some of the writing is smooth. Many sentences do not flow smoothly.
1 Huh?	❑ The writing is not organized at all. ❑ It does not fit the writer's purpose.	❑ The sentences do not flow smoothly or logically.

Name _____   Date _____

Main Idea and Details Diagram

Write the old object you chose in the box at the top. Write about details that support the main idea in the smaller boxes.

Main idea

Detail　　　　**Detail**　　　　**Detail**

Writing Project

Revise

Use revision marks to make changes to this letter. Look for:
- **parts of the letter**
- **specific words**

Revision Marks	
∧	Add
ℐ	Take out
⭘⟋	Move to here

January 10

Dear Maria,

my grandpa took me to a show. One car was older

than him! That old car had skinny wheels. It did not have

seatbelts. I think that old car is not safe.

Keiko

Writing Project

Edit and Proofread

Use revision marks to edit and proofread this letter. Look for:

- correct spelling of silent consonants
- words that sound alike
- correct use of past and future verbs
- a capital letters on names and months

Revision Marks	
^	Add
ℑ	Take out
◯ SP	Check spelling
=	Capitalize

january 10

Dear maria,

Grandma Rose take me to a store last week. It had a sine that said

"Out of the Past." We saw an old ink pen that people used to rite in

school. They called it a fountain pen. You have to put the ink in it. She

said she had one at school when she was little. I think it must have

been very messy. She said she show me how to use one next week.

Your friend,

Keiko

Unit Concept Map

Get Out the Map!

Make a concept map with the answers to the Big Question:
Why do we need maps?

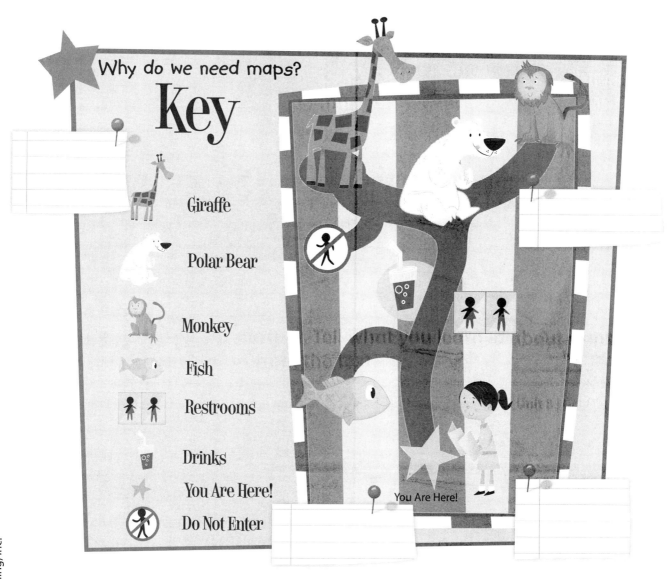

Use Information

Draw symbols and signs that you see in town. Then write what they mean in the column on the right.

Symbols and signs	What they mean

Find the Adverb!

Grammar Rules **Adverbs That Tell How**

1. An **adverb** can tell how something happens.
2. These **adverbs** end in **-ly**.
   Example: *She spoke **slowly**.*

Underline the verb in each sentence. Circle the adverb.

1. Jim looked carefully at the map.

2. Lisa asked loudly for directions.

3. She kindly gave us directions.

4. We were finally on our way.

5. We turned quickly around the corner.

6. My mom drove slowly in front of my friend's house.

Work with a partner. Put adverb word cards in a paper bag. Take turns drawing adverbs out of the bag. Use each adverb in a sentence and act it out.

Name _____   Date _____

"If Maps Could Talk"

Listen as your teacher reads. Follow with your finger.

1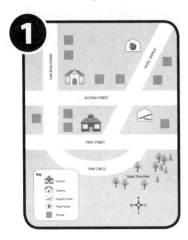

Maps use symbols to show where things are. Read the key to learn the meanings of map symbols.

2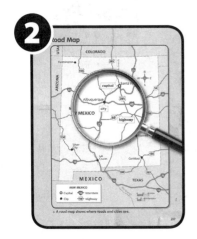

Symbols on a road map help drivers find their way. Symbols on a weather map show what the weather will be.

3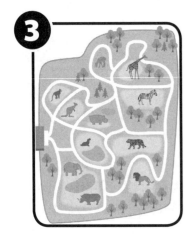

Some maps don't have keys. These maps use picture symbols of real things.

Grammar

Where? When?

> **Grammar Rules** Adverbs That Tell Where, When
>
> 1. Some **adverbs** tell **where** something happens.
>   Example: *We turned **left**.*
> 2. Some **adverbs** tell **when** something happens.
>   Example: *We will arrive **tomorrow**.*

1. Toss a marker onto one of the adverbs below.
2. Use the adverb in a sentence. Create as many sentences as you can.
3. Take turns with a partner.
4. The player who writes the most correct sentences wins.

there	later
today	nearby
yesterday	away
everywhere	first
next	here

Take turns with a partner. Read aloud two of your sentences.

Around the World

Play a game using Key Words.

1. The traveler stands behind a challenger.

2. The challenger listens to the traveler's clue and names the Key Word.

3. The traveler moves behind the next student on the right if the challenger answers correctly. The first traveler to go all around the circle wins.

Symbol!

KEY WORDS

map	key	meaning	symbol	picture	useful

CLUES

- A _____ can be a shape or picture.

- A _____ tells the meaning of a map's symbols.

- A map is _____ for finding places.

- He drew a _____ of a house.

- Look on the _____ to find the library.

- A key shows the _____ of a symbol or sign.

Reread and Retell

Symbols and Signs

Draw symbols and signs from "If Maps Could Talk." Write their meanings in the column on the right.

Symbols and signs	What they mean
	• mostly sunny
	•
	•

Take turns with a partner. Tell what you learned about signs, symbols, and maps from the text.

Phonics Practice

Vowel Sounds and Spellings: *oi, oy*

c<u>oi</u>n

b<u>oy</u>

Read each word. Circle the word that goes with each picture.

1.	2.
voice vote vice	poster oyster older
3.	**4.**
loyal local label	oat oil open
5.	**6.**
pin pant point	toy toe told

Work with a partner. Take turns reading the sentence and pointing to the objects.

Find a toy, some oil, and an oyster.

Fluency

"If Maps Could Talk"

Use this passage to practice reading with proper phrasing.

Step 1

2

Draw the outline of your school. Show what

10

your school would look like from above.

17

Step 2

19

Draw your classroom as a square.

25

Put a symbol in the classroom, such as a star.

35

Step 3

37

Draw other rooms in your school, like the

45

cafeteria. Add hallways, restrooms, and doors.

51

From "If Maps Could Talk," page 236

Phrasing

B ☐ Rarely pauses while reading text.

A ☐ Frequently pauses at appropriate points in the text.

I ☐ Occasionally pauses while reading text.

AH ☐ Consistently pauses at all appropriate points in the text.

Accuracy and Rate Formula

Use the formula to measure a reader's accuracy and rate while reading aloud.

_____ – _____ = _____

words attempted in one minute   number of errors   words correct per minute (wcpm)

Compare Genres

Compare an informational text and a poem.

Informational text	Poem
gives definitions	uses words to create images in your mind

▱▱▱ **Take turns with a partner. Ask questions about an informational text and a poem.**

Grammar

Trip to the Train Station

Grammar Rules Adverbs

Adverbs can tell:

- **how** something happens.
- **where** something happens.
- **when** something happens.

Read the passage. Categorize the underlined adverbs in the chart below.

My grandfather and I walked <u>quickly</u> to the train station. We turned <u>left</u> at the corner. <u>Then</u> we turned <u>right</u> on Park Street. The train will arrive <u>soon</u>. We are waiting patiently.

Adverbs		
Where	**How**	**When**
_____	quickly	_____
_____	_____	_____
_____	_____	_____
_____	_____	_____

With a partner, add more adverbs to the chart. Use one of the adverbs in a sentence.

Thinking Map

Identify Problem and Solution

Tell a different story about Jack. Imagine Jack is with a friend. Complete the problem-and-solution chart.

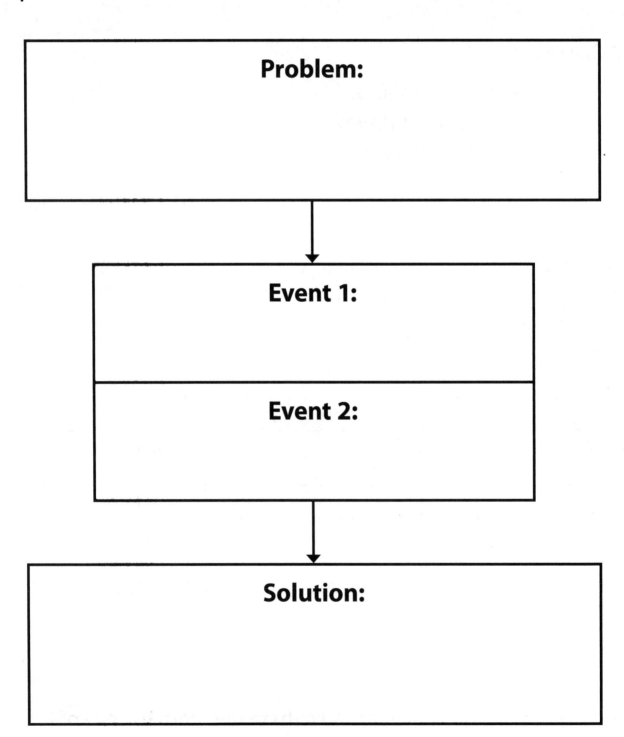

Problem:

Event 1:

Event 2:

Solution:

Grammar

Where Is It?

Grammar Rules Prepositions Tell Where, Show Direction

1. **Prepositions** can tell where things are.

   Example: *My house is **next to** a par*k.

2. **Prepositions** can tell a direction, or a way to go.

   Example: *My mom and I walk **to** the park.*

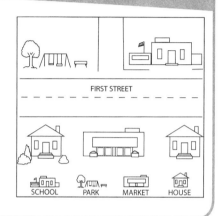

Read each sentence. Look at the map. Circle the correct word or phrase. Then complete the sentence.

1. A school is <u>on</u> First Street.   (on) in

2. A market is _____ the houses.   inside between

3. A house is _____ from the school.   around across

4. A park is _____ the school.   next to into

▸ **Look at the map. Write a new sentence using a preposition. Read it to a partner.**

"Little Red Riding Hood"

Listen as your teacher reads. Follow with your finger.

Little Red Riding Hood lived in a village south of a forest. Her Grandma was sick. Little Red Riding Hood went to visit her. She took a map with her.

Little Red Riding Hood followed her map. Suddenly, Big Bad Wolf came out of the forest. He wanted to eat Little Red Riding Hood. But people were walking on the path. Then he had an idea.

The wolf looked at his map. He found a different way to Grandma's house. He put Grandma in the closet. He put on her nightgown. He pretended he was Grandma. He was going to eat Little Red Riding Hood!

Little Red Riding Hood got to Grandma's house. She looked inside. She saw two long ears, a very long nose, and two black eyes. That wasn't Grandma! She went to the farmer's house. She asked for help. The wolf saw the farmer. The wolf jumped out of the window and ran away.

Grammar

On My Desk

Grammar Rules Prepositional Phrases

A **prepositional phrase** is a small group of words.

Begin a **prepositional phrase** with a **preposition**.

Example: *The teacher walks **around the desk***.

Read the sentence. Circle the preposition. Underline the prepositional phrase.

1. I walk (to) my desk.

2. There is a book on my desk.

3. My bag is next to my chair.

4. A pencil fell under my desk.

5. I walk out of the classroom.

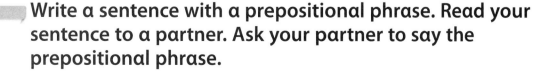
Write a sentence with a prepositional phrase. Read your sentence to a partner. Ask your partner to say the prepositional phrase.

Vocabulary

Picture It

1. **Form pairs. Choose a pair to be the artists and a pair to be the guessers.**

2. **The artists secretly select a Key Word.**

3. **The artists draw a picture to show the word's meaning**

4. **The guessers guess which Key Word the picture shows.**

5. **Switch roles.**

KEY WORDS

path	north	south	east	west	near
left	right	location	direction	far	follow

1.	2.
3.	4.

Keeping Score

If the guessers answer correctly, they get one point.
The first pair to get three points wins!

Name _____ Date _____

Problem-and-Solution Chart

Write a sentence about the problem in "Little Red Riding Hood." Then list the main events in the story. Lastly, write a sentence that tells how the problem is solved.

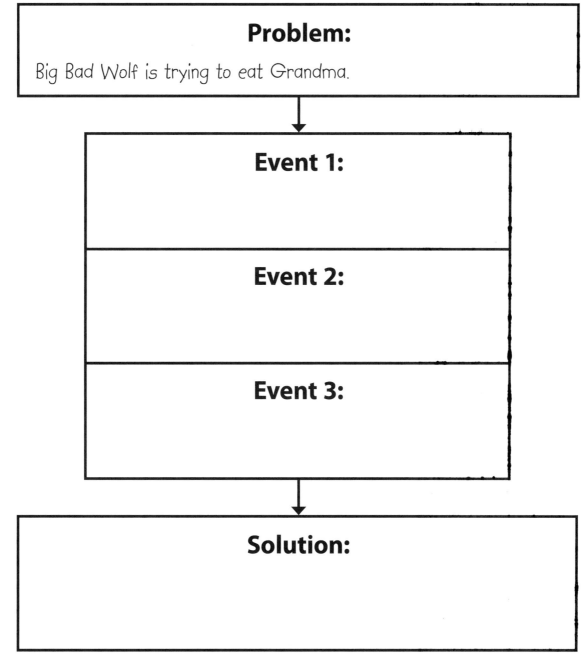

Problem:

Big Bad Wolf is trying to eat Grandma.

Event 1:

Event 2:

Event 3:

Solution:

Use your problem-and-solution chart to retell the story to a partner.

Phonics Practice

Vowel Sounds and Spellings:
OU, OW

cl<u>ou</u>d   c<u>ow</u>

Read each word. Circle the word that goes with each picture.

1.	hose house his	**2.**	oil old owl
3.	road rind round	**4.**	groan grind ground
5.	plow plan plum	**6.**	clan clown clean

Work with a partner. Take turns reading the sentence.

The clown and his owl live in the house down the road.

Fluency

"Little Red Riding Hood"

Use this passage to practice reading with proper expression.

One day, Little Red Riding Hood's mother   7
said, "Grandmother is sick. Take her some   14
food. Visit with her for a while."   21

"Yes, Mom," Little Red Riding Hood said.   28
"I will go now."   32

"Follow the shortest path. Do not get   39
distracted. Go quickly!" her mother said.   45
"Do not forget your map."   50

"Yes, Mom. I will take the map with   58
me," said Little Red Riding Hood.   64

From "Little Red Riding Hood," pages 256–257

Expression

[B] ☐ Does not read with feeling.   [A] ☐ Reads with appropriate feeling for most content.

[I] ☐ Reads with some feeling, but does not match content.   [AH] ☐ Reads with appropriate feeling for all content.

Accuracy and Rate Formula

Use the formula to measure a reader's accuracy and rate while reading aloud.

_____ − _____ = _____
words attempted   number of errors   words correct per minute
in one minute   (wcpm)

Compare Genres

Compare a fairy tale and a how-to article.

Fairy tale	How-to article
tells a story that cannot happen in real life	tells how to make something that is real

Take turns with a partner. Tell how a fairy tale and a how-to article are different.

Grammar

The Preposition Game

Grammar Rules Prepositions

Prepositions can tell where. Put prepositions before a noun that names a place.

Examples:

*The book is **on** the **table**.*

*The clock is **next to** the map.*

next to	across	between	under

| at | | | down |

START

1. Play with a partner.
2. Use a small object for a game piece.
3. Flip a coin.

   = Move one space.

   = Move two spaces.

in

4. Use the preposition in a sentence.
5. Write the prepositional phrase on another sheet of paper.

over

FINISH

6. The first one to reach FINISH wins!

into	on	above	up

Writing Project

Ideas

Writing is well-developed when the **message** is clear and **interesting** to the reader. It is supported by **details** that show the writer knows the topic well.

	Is the message clear and focused?	Do the details show the writer knows the topic?
4 Wow!	❑ All of the writing is clear and focused.	❑ All the details are about the topic. The writer knows the topic well.
3 Ahh.	❑ Most of the writing is clear and focused.	❑ Most of the details are about the topic. The writer knows the topic fairly well.
2 Hmm.	❑ Some of the writing is not clear. The writing lacks some focus.	❑ Some details are about the topic. The writer doesn't know the topic well.
1 Huh?	❑ The writing is not clear or focused.	❑ Many details are not about the topic. The writer does not know the topic.

Problem-and-Solution Chart

Write the story problem in the top box. Write the events that happen in the middle boxes. Write the solution in the bottom box.

Problem:

Event 1:

Event 2:

Solution:

Writing Project

Revise

Use revision marks to make changes to this literary response. Look for:

- a story title
- a problem
- a solution
- an opinion about the story
- varied sentences

Revision Marks	
∧	Add
℘	Take out
⌒⌐	Move to here

I read "A New Old Tune" by Pat Cummings. Max helps his Aunt

Nell get ready for a yard sale. He finds some some old things. One

thing he finds is a record. Max doesn't know what it is or how to

play it. Aunt Nell and Max dance I like this story

Writing Project

Edit and Proofread

Use revision marks to edit and proofread this literary response. Look for:

- **correct spelling of prefixes and suffixes**
- **capital letters at beginning of sentences**
- **correct adverbs and prepositions**

Revision Marks	
^	Add
℘	Take out
⬭	Check spelling
≡	Capitalize

The Three Little Pigs

by Pin-mei Yau

I read The "Three Little Pigs." a big, bad wolf wanted to eat the three little pigs.

The pigs quickle built three houses. The wolf blew down the unnsafe houses of straw and sticks. the wolf could not blow the brick house down, and he left in a quickly.

The three little pigs were safe of the brick house. i think the wolf leaving made "The Three Little Pigs" a good story.

Photographic Credits

5.14 (t) BirdImages/Getty Images. (c) mattabbe/Getty Images. (b) x-posure/Getty Images. 7.4 (t) CRG STUDIOS/ Getty Images. (tc) Lester Lefkowitz/Getty Images. (tc) Giakita/Shutterstock.com. (bc) Fotosearch/Getty Images. (bc) Adrio/iStock/Getty Images. (bc) SYUJI NISHIDA/amana images/Getty Images. (bc) Bettmann/ Getty Images. (b) Elizabeth Alice Austen/Library of Congress. (b) Old Paper Studios/Alamy Stock Photo. (b) sjlocke/Deposit Photos. (b) David Young-Wolff/PhotoEdit.